Wild Animals

Factastic

Coloring Book

Table of Contents

Written by Jonathan Briden
Illustrated by Bogdan Enache

ISBN: 978-1-4960-5830-0

http://www.jonathanbriden.com

Animals
of
Africa

Africa is a very large continent, made up of more than 50 different countries.

With everything from arid deserts to dense jungles, and high mountain peaks to the wide open savannah, Africa provides the right home for a huge variety of animals.

Some of the world's biggest and most majestic land animals call Africa home. In fact, there are over 1,100 separate species of mammals in Africa. There are also more than 2,600 types of bird, hundreds of species of amphibians and reptiles, and hundreds of thousands of species of insects.

African Elephant

The African Elephant is much larger than his Asian cousin. A large male, or bull, elephant stands 13ft (4m) tall at the shoulder, and can weigh over 13,000lb (6,000kg).

It's not easy to get so big, and a large elephant can eat up to 1,000lb (450kg) of leaves, grass, bark and fruit every day.

Elephants are also very, very smart. They have a bigger brain than any other land animal, and are considered to be just as smart as chimpanzees, gorillas, whales, and dolphins.

For a long time elephants have been poached for their ivory, and are still at risk in many parts of Africa.

Cheetah

Cheetahs are the fastest land animal, and can reach speeds of up to 75 miles an hour (120 kilometres per hour). They have powerful hind legs, a large chest, and narrow waist. They can also turn very quickly when chasing prey, such as gazelles, using their long tail like a rudder.

Female cheetahs tend to live alone, except when raising their cubs. Male cheetahs prefer to group together, and often stay with their brothers for their whole life.

Cheetahs were once common right across Africa and parts of Asia, but their numbers have been greatly diminished due to hunting.

Lion

Lions are often referred to as the "King of the Beasts", and they certainly are a magnificent looking animal.

A male can weigh over 550lb (250kg), and they are the tallest (at the shoulder) of all the cats. But, lions are not the heaviest nor the longest cat. Do you know which is?

As big and powerful as he is, the male lion generally does not hunt, but stays and looks after the cubs while the female lions go out to hunt.

Lions mainly eat wildebeest, zebras, buffalo, and warthogs.

Gorilla

Gorillas are the largest of the great apes, weighing up to 400lb (180kg). They live in dense forests where they can find the lush green plants they like to eat.

Gorillas sleep on the ground, building a nest out of branches and leaves.

Although Gorillas mainly eat plants, they will happily gulp down ants and termites when they find them.

Gorillas are very intelligent, and have a wide range of different sounds and calls that they use for communicating with each other.

Lemur

Lemurs live on the island of Madagascar off the coast of Southeast Africa. They come in all sorts of shapes and sizes. Madame Berthe's mouse lemur is the smallest, weighing just 1.2oz (30g). and the biggest are the Indri which can weigh 21lb (9.5kg).

Hundreds of years ago there were even bigger lemurs, the largest of which was bigger than a gorilla!

Lemurs have a very good sense of smell, which they use to find their favorite foods. Different types of lemurs eat different things. Many small lemurs eat insects and fruit, whereas larger lemurs mostly eat plants.

Baboon

Baboons have long, dog-like muzzles, powerful jaws and sharp teeth. They mostly eat plants and fruit, but will also eat insects and occasionally catch fish, hares, birds, or other small animals to eat.

Baboons are found on the savannah, in open woodland and on hills across Africa. They spend most of their time on the ground, but are good climbers and will climb trees or cliffs to escape from predators, or to find a safe place to sleep.

Baboons live in groups called "troops". A troop may contain just a few baboons, or as many as 250. Most troops have around 50 animals.

Zebra

Zebras are related to horses, but have distinctive black and white stripes. Some scientists believe they help camouflage the animals in long grass. Others say that the stripes are confusing to predators (like lions) when the animals move. One study even showed that having stripes makes zebras attract fewer flies.

But are zebras white with black stripes or black with white stripes? Scientists found the answer by looking at the way baby zebras develop. They start off black and the white stripes come later - so the answer is black with white stripes.

Zebras eat grass, but always have to be on the lookout for dangerous predators like lions. Luckily they have excellent eyesight and hearing. If one zebra sees or hears a lion he makes a loud noise to warn all the other zebras.

Giraffe

Giraffes can be up to 20 feet tall (6m), with their long necks and long legs allowing them to reach their favorite food - acacia leaves. Acacia trees are very spiky, but giraffes have a very long, strong tongue that they wrap around the leaves to pull them away.

The dappled pattern of a giraffe acts as camouflage, mimicking the patchy light of the sun shining down through the trees of the forest. Every giraffe's coat pattern is unique, which means you'll never find two giraffes that look exactly the same.

Because if it's great height, a giraffe's heart has to be very strong to pump blood all the way up to the brain. The heart can weigh up to 25lb (11kg) which is about 1% of the total weight of the giraffe.

Ostrich

Ostriches are very tall, flightless birds, with long necks and long legs. They are the fastest bird on land, and can run at 40 miles an hour (70kph). They also lay the largest egg of any bird, and have the largest eye of any land animal - 2 inches diameter (5cm).

They have excellent vision and excellent hearing which helps them in avoiding predators like lions and hyenas. If an ostrich becomes cornered it will kick with it's powerful legs.

Ostriches mostly eat seeds, grass, fruit, and flowers, but will also eat insects like locusts. They have no teeth to chew their food, and swallow small pebbles that help to grind up food in their gizzard.

Hippopotamus

The word "hippopotamus" comes from Greek and means "river horse". They do sometimes live in rivers, but you certainly wouldn't want to try to put a saddle on one. Hippos are one of the most dangerous animals in Africa, can weigh around 4,400lb (2,000kg), and have even been known to kill crocodiles!

When a hippo opens its mouth really wide, it's not yawning. It's a sign the hippo is angry, and may be about to attack.

Although they are aggressive, hippos are herbivores, meaning they only eat plants. They spend most of the day in the water, but they don't eat very many water-plants. They come out of the water at night to eat grass, and can eat 150lb of grass (68kg) every night.

Rhinoceros

There are two types of rhino in Africa. They are called the White Rhino and the Black Rhino, but really all rhinos are gray.

Rhinos can weigh up to 5,000lb (2,400kg), and are renowned for being quite bad tempered. Partly this is due to them having very poor eyesight, so that they respond aggressively to anything that they think might be a threat. Due to their large size, frightening horns, and aggressive nature, they have no natural predators.

Sadly though they are hunted and killed for their horns.

African Buffalo

African buffalos are a very large, weighing up to 2,000lb (900kg). They have large curved horns that join at the base. They live together in large herds and they help to protect each other, often chasing off or even killing lions when they attack.

In one famous video, a calf is attacked by a group of lions and then a crocodile as well, but the herd attack the lions and rescue the calf.

During resting periods, female buffalos "vote" on where to go next by sitting facing in the direction they want to go. When it comes time to move, the whole herd moves in the direction with the most votes.

Spotted Hyena

Hyenas look similar to dogs, but they are more closely related to cats. They have very powerful jaws, strong enough to crush and eat bones. When hyenas eat, they eat almost the entire animal.

Hyenas live in large groups, called "clans", with up to 80 animals in a group. The female spotted hyena is larger than the male, and within the clan, the females are in charge.

Hyenas are well known for their laugh, but also have a large range of other sounds that they use to communicate including whoops, grunts, groans, lows, giggles, yells, growls, grunt-laughs, whines, and squeals.

Nile Crocodile

Nile crocodiles can reach over 18 feet (5.5m) in length, and have very powerful jaws and sharp teeth. A crocodile's eyes and nostrils are near the top of its head allowing it to remain almost completely submerged so it can ambush animals when they come down to drink.

Crocodiles lay around 50 eggs, similar in size to chicken eggs, but with a thinner shell. The female buries them in the sand near the river and then guards the eggs for 3 months until they hatch.

If the temperature in the nest is between 89.1°F (31.7°C) and 94.1°F (34.5°C), then the baby crocodiles will all be males. If the temperature is higher or lower then the baby crocodiles will all be female.

Animals of Asia

Asia is the largest continent, covering 30% of its total land area. In Asia, you will find every kind of landscape - The world's tallest mountains (the Himalayas), arid deserts, dense jungles, and tropical islands.

Asia is home to a great variety of amazing animals too - From the lovable giant panda, to the magnificent tiger, and the terrifying Komodo dragon.

Asia also has more people than anywhere else. 60% of the world's population lives in Asia. Deforestation, farming, and other human activities pose many risks to the animals that live there.

Giant Panda

The giant panda is a bear that lives in China. Unlike other bears, the panda is almost exclusively herbivorous with more than 99% of its food coming from bamboo.

A panda has an unusual paw with five fingers plus a thumb. It uses its thumbs to help grip bamboo when eating. Because bamboo is not very nutritious, a panda has to eat a lot – up to 30lb (14kg) every day.

The giant panda is an endangered species. Pandas have a very low birth rate, and its specialized diet of bamboo makes pandas very vulnerable to loss of habitat to farming and other human activities.

Tiger

Tigers are the largest of the big cats. The biggest tigers are Siberian tigers which can weigh up to 675lb (306kg) and can be 91 inches (230cm) long - not including the tail.

Tigers mostly live alone, and hunt deer, wild boar, and water buffalo. They will also attack domestic animals such as cattle and horses. Sometimes old or wounded tigers, that can no longer catch wild prey, will turn to hunting humans, but generally tigers try to stay away from people.

Tigers used to be abundant, but have been wiped out in many areas, and are endangered in all the remaining areas where they still live.

Clouded Leopard

The clouded leopard lives in the foothills of the Himalayas. They have an irregular blotchy patterned coat, which helps keeped them hidden in their forest habitat, although they are sometimes spotted very high up in the mountains.

Clouded leopards are considered to be the best climbers of all cats. They can climb down a vertical tree-trunk head-first, hang from a branch using only their back feet and tail, and even climb along a horizontal branch upside-down.

At night, they hunt for hog-deer, porcupines, ground squirrels and other small prey.

Orangutan

Orangutans are a member of the great ape family that live in the rainforests of Borneo and Sumatra. They spend most of their time in the trees looking for fruit to eat. They also eat leaves, insects, honey, and birds eggs.

Orangutans are one of the most intelligent animals. They carefully construct nests, one for daytime use and another for nighttime. Young orangutans watch their mother to learn this skill.

Orangutans also make use of tools for getting insects out of tree hollows, and other tools for extracting the seeds from fruit. They also use leaves to amplify the kiss-squeak sounds that they use for communicating.

Asian Elephant

Asian elephants are not as big as their African cousins, have smaller ears, and are generally quite timid. This allowed people in Asia to capture and train them to help with tasks such as lifting and carrying heavy objects.

An elephant's trunk contains as many as 60,000 muscles. It is incredibly strong and flexible and is used for many tasks including breathing, making sounds, drinking, feeding, touching, dusting, and washing.

Asian elephants are very smart and exhibit many signs of intelligence, including the use of tools, cooperation, learning, memory, emotion, self-awareness, and language.

Komodo Dragon

The Komodo dragon is a very large monitor lizard - up to 10ft (3m) long. They live on the island of Komodo and a few other islands, all in Indonesia.

Komodo dragons have extremely tough skin, reinforced by armored scales, and lots of very sharp teeth. They mostly eat animals that are already dead, but also sometimes ambush prey. They eat a variety of animals, and will swallow smaller animals, up to the size of a goat, whole.

A Komodo dragon can eat 80% of its own weight in one meal. With such large amounts of food, they may only need to feed once a month.

Indian Cobra

The Indian cobra is a medium-sized snake with a distinctive hooded neck. When the snake feels threatened he raises up his head and expands the hood to appear larger.

Cobras are venomous and responsible for a lot of snakebites in India. If the bite is not treated it may result in death. Cobras only bite people when they feel threatened. They normally eat rodents, frogs, other small animals, and eggs.

They are a popular choice for snake-charmers. The cobra cannot hear the snake charmer's flute, but is responding to the movement of the instrument.

Animals
of
Australia

Australia is both a country and a continent. Some people refer to it as the "island continent". Being isolated for a long time from the other major landmasses it has some very unusual animals that exist nowhere else.

Many of Australia's mammals are marsupials, which means they carry their young in a pouch, and Australia is also home to the only monotremes - the platypus and echidna - mammals that lay eggs.

Australian animals are so strange, that when European explorers first sent stuffed specimens back to Europe, people thought they were fakes.

Kangaroo

Kangaroos are Australian marsupials and raise their young in a pouch. They have very large, powerful back legs and can leap long distances. They use their large muscular tail for balancing.

Kangaroos usually live together in groups, called "mobs". They are very good swimmers, and if threatened by a dingo they will often try to escape into water. If the dingo follows, a large kangaroo will use its front paws to hold the dingo under the water to drown it.

Kangaroos eat grass and shrubs, and often have to travel long distances to find food and water. The way that they hop is very efficient allowing them to cover long distances without tiring.

Koala

Koalas may look like a teddy bear, but like the kangaroo and many other Australian mammals they are also marsupials.

Koalas feed almost exclusively on gum leaves. Gum leaves are hard to digest and do not provide much energy. As a result koalas sleep up to 20 hours a day and spend much of their awake time eating.

When a koala is born it is tiny, just 0.02oz (0.5g), and must crawl into its mother's pouch to finish developing. It takes another 6 months before the baby koala is developed enough to poke his head out of the mother's pouch.

Wombat

The wombat is another Australian marsupial that wouldn't look out of place in a toy store. Their closest relative is the koala. Wombats eat grasses, herbs, bark, and roots. They have a stocky build and weigh up to 77lb (35kg).

Unlike most other marsupials, wombats have a backwards facing pouch. When a wombat digs its large burrow it wouldn't want a pouch full of dirt!

If a wombat it threatened by a predator it runs into its burrow. They have a very tough back end, and no tail, making it difficult for a predator to grab hold of them.

Platypus

The platypus is one of the strangest mammals you will ever meet. It has a bill like a duck, feet like an otter, and a tail like a beaver - and it lays eggs! Not only that but male platypuses have a venomous spur that they use for defence.

If all that's not weird enough, they are also one of the only mammals able to use electrolocation - finding their prey by sensing the electrical impulses generated by muscle movement.

Platypus live in and around streams, and rivers. They build a small burrow in the river bank, but spend much of their time in the water looking for worms, shrimp, and insect larvae.

Bilby

Bilbies are another very cute Australian marsupial. They have a long nose, large ears, silky fur and a long tail. They eat insects, spiders, fruit, fungi, and bulbs. They get all the water they need from their food and do not need to drink water.

Their large ears give them good hearing for detecting predators, and also help keep the bilby cool by letting out heat.

Bilbies are excellent burrowers. They build up to a dozen burrows, so they always have one close to escape from predators or to shelter from the heat of the day. Like the wombat, the female has a rear-facing pouch to avoid getting dirt in it.

Brushtail Possum

Brushtail possums are one of the most common marsupials in Australia. They spend most of their time in trees and eat leaves, flowers, fruits, and seeds. They sometimes also eat insects and birds eggs.

The tail of the brushtail possum is very fluffy but has no fur underneath. This helps the possum to use its tail to grip branches when moving through the trees.

Possums have adapted well to living in urban areas, and can be very noisy, especially at night, making a variety of sounds including screeches, clicks, grunts, hisses, alarm chatters, and coughing sounds.

Tasmanian Devil

The Tasmanian devil is about the size of a small dog but is the largest carnivorous marsupial. It kills and eats other small animals, and also scavenges. For its size, it has one of the strongest bites if any mammal.

It gets its name from its ferocious eating behaviour and the loud screeching sounds it makes.

Tasmanian devils have a stocky build, but are surprisingly fast runners, excellent swimmers, and can climb trees. They have excellent hearing and a very good sense of smell.